I See You!

by Lada Josefa Kratky

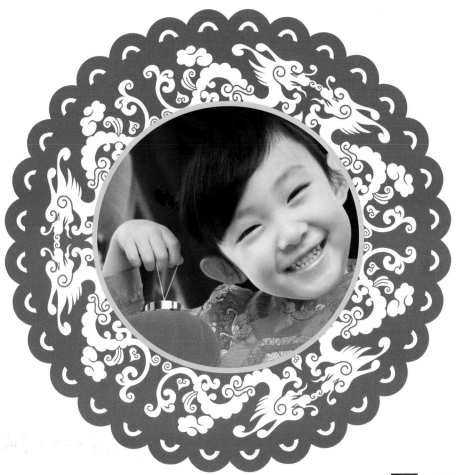

NATIONAL GEOGRAPHIC

School Publishing

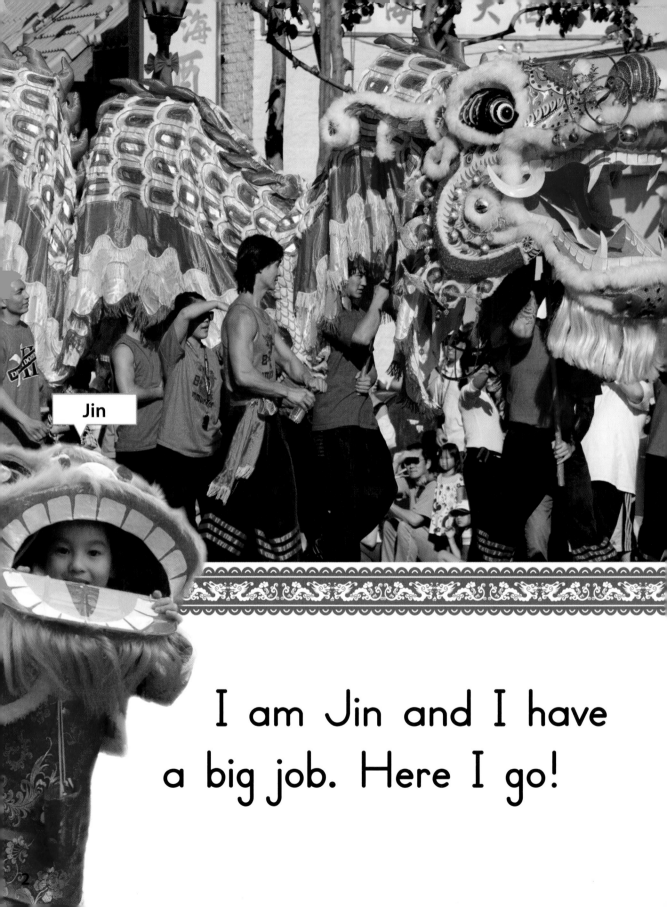

Jin

I am Jin and I have a big job. Here I go!

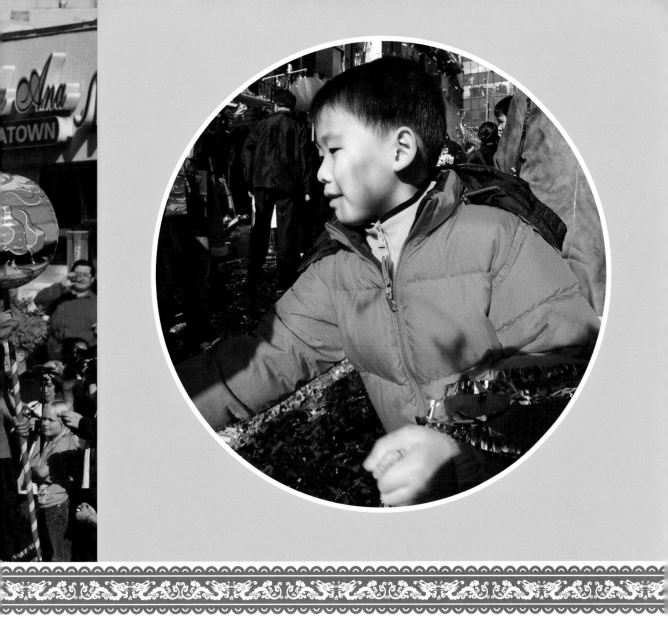

I see Bill and he sees me.

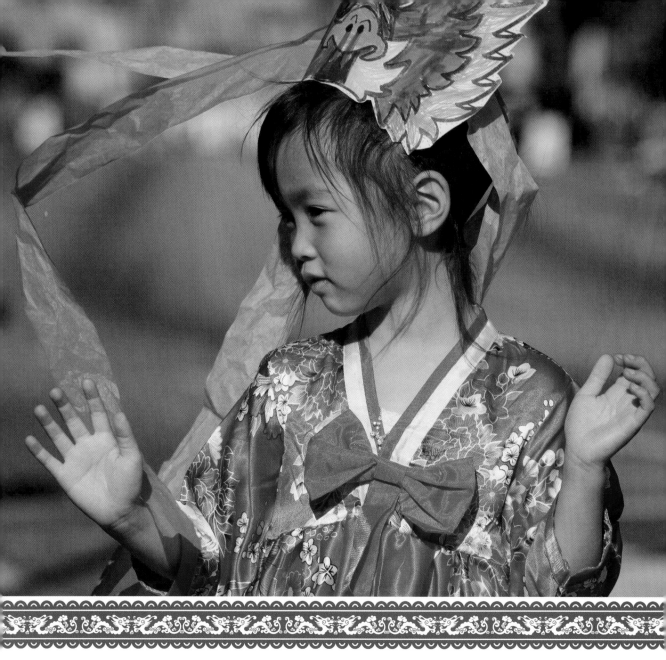

I see Meg and she sees me.

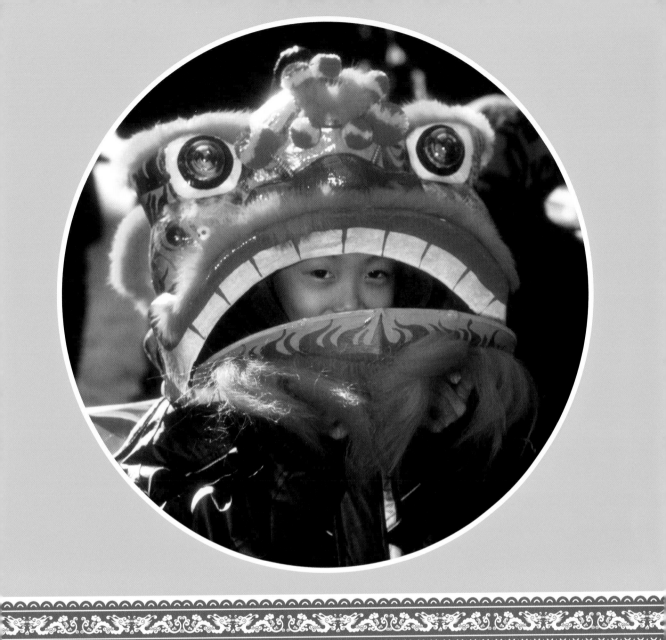

I see Jeb and he sees me.

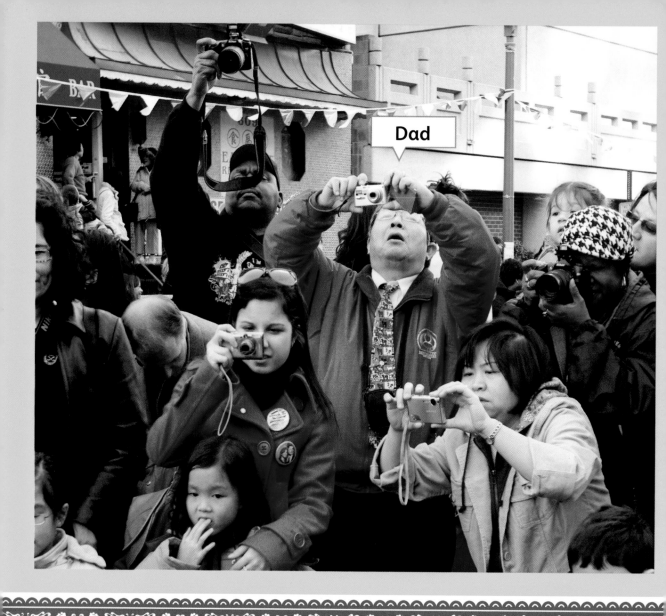

I see Dad and he sees me.

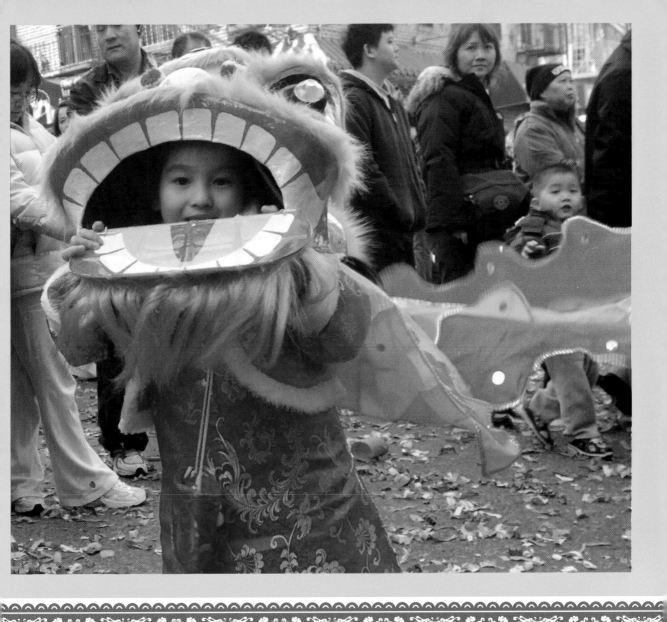

Dad! Here I am!

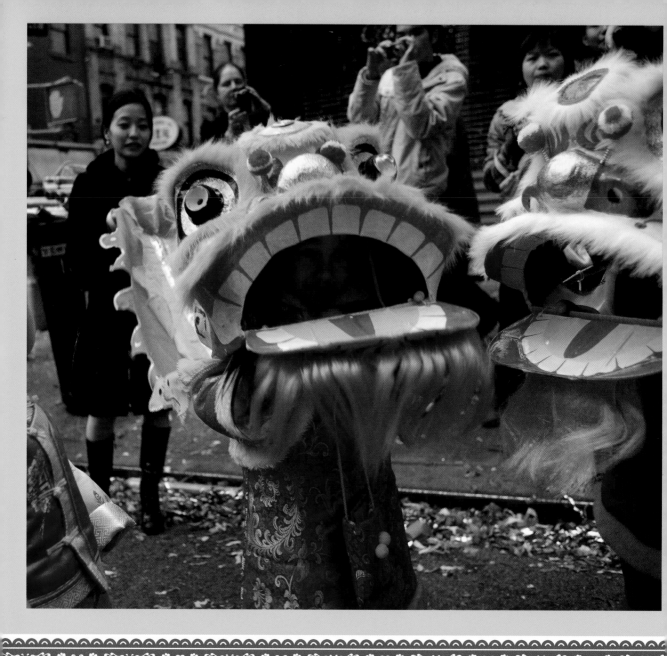

I see you!